Types Of Poetry

Rhymes To Thyme

ALBERT F. SCHMID

Ordering Information:

For orders and inquiries, please contact:
1-888-375-9818
www.toplinkpublishing.com
bookorder@toplinkpublishing.com

Printed in the United States of America

CONTENTS

We do not find the meaning of life
By ourselves alone—we find it with others.
Thank you, Beverly Baird and Sheri Litchfield,
for all of your help.

POETRY

The term **Poetry** comes from a Greek word, *poiesis,* which means "making" and is a form of literature that uses aesthetic and rhythmic qualities of language. Phonesthetics, sound symbolism and metre all have ways of effecting the meaning in addition to, or in place of the prosaic meaning.

Poetry has a long history, dating back to the Sumerian Epic of Gilgamesh. Early poems developed from folk songs, or the need to tell a story or an event. Ancient attempts to define poetry, such as Aristotle's *Poetics,* focused on the use of speech in rhetoric drama, song and comedy. Later attempts considered features such as repetition of words, verse form and rhyme. From the 20th century, poetry has generally been regarded as a fundamental creative act, using language.

Poetry uses forms and methods to suggest various interpretations to words or to evoke emotive response. Devices like assonance, alliteration, onomatopoeia and rhythm are often used to achieve musical or incantatory effects.

Some poetry types are specific to the cultures and genres and are effective in the language with which the author uses. Readers often identify with the poets if the poem is written in lines based on rhyme and regular meter. Biblical poetry may not use a rhyme but a rhythm and euphony. Poets today, in the globalizing world often adapt forms, styles and techniques taken from diverse cultures and languages.

The oldest surviving poem, the *Epic of Gilgamesh,* comes from the 3rd millennium BCE in Sumer (now Iraq), and was written on clay tablets and later papyrus. The tablets place the date as 2000 BC. The poem describes an antique rite in which the King symbolically married and mated with the goddess Inanna to ensure fertility and prosperity.

Albert F. Schmid

WHAT IS A POEM

Webster defines a poem as an arrangement of words written or spoken: traditionally a rhythmical composition, sometimes rhymed expressing experiences, or emotions in a style more consecrated, imaginative, and powerful than that of ordinary speech or prose. Some poems are in meter, some in free verse.

A poet is one who writes poetry or verses. Poets display imaginative power and qualities, emotions, and beauty of thought with descriptive language Subjects of poems are as varied as the writer. Some poets specialize in different themes. One of the most popular is the subject of Love. William Shakespeare is famous for his sonnets on Love. There are inspirational poems by William Henley and Edgar Allan Poe.

There are inspirational poems written by William Henley and Rudyard Kipling and poems concerned with death and disillusionment by A. E. Housman and Edward Arlington Robinson. Some poems are deeply personal while others are profoundly political. Ralph Waldo Emerson, Henry Wadsworth Longfellow, Alfred Lord Emerson are represented by poems of deeply patriotic concepts.

Vincent Millay relates stories in a straight forward narrative, while Matthew Arnold and Robert Frost have written about fundamental human experience. Poetry by William Blake and Joyce Kilmer look to divine authority.

Many poems share a similar theme, but each is an individual work with a specific message, individualized through the means by which the poet uses his words; Metaphors, allusions, symbolism, and rhyme scheme to elaborate the message.

All suggest a world much greater than can be encompassed within their words, and the way in which they impact the reader and challenge his thinking.

HOW TO WRITE POETRY

Writing poetry is about observing the world within and around you. A poem can be about anything, about love, about a trip, about a special event, about a loss or even a death. Sad or glad. Writing poetry can seem daunting, especially if you do not feel naturally creative. With the right inspiration and approach, you can write a poem that you will be proud to share with others in your social circle or family.

Starting the Poem. Do writing exercises. Start with a snipper or a versus. A line or two may come out of thin air. Grab a note book or go to your computer and write it down. Let your mind wander for 5-10 minutes and see what comes up.

Get inspired by your environment. Go for a walk. Sit on the shore or go to the park. Let the things you see, the people you meet, the nature you observe be inspirational. Write about someone you care about. Think of someone who is important to you like a dear friend, or your spouse, or a parent and recall a special moment that you have shared with them. Strong emotional moments make for beautiful, interesting poems.

Pick a specific theme or idea. You may have a specific theme you can use to focus on to give your poem a clear goal or purpose. This helps narrow down the images and descriptions you will use. Try to be specific when you choose a theme or idea.

Choose a poetic form. There are many different poetic forms that you can use from free verse to sonnet to rhyming couplet. Go for a form that you find easy to use and stay with it. You may opt for a form that is funny or playful such as a limerick. You may go for a lyrical form like a sonnet, or the ballad form, or go to a rhyming couplet for a dramatic or romantic poem.

Read examples of poetry. To get a better idea of what other poets are writing you may look for examples of poetry. You may find a writer who challenges your creative senses. You may find a well-known poem that is considered "classics" to get a better sense of the genre. For example:

"The Red Wheelbarrow" by William Carlos Williams.

Writing the Poem. Avoid abstract imagery and go for absolute descriptions. Try to describe people, places, and things in the poem using the five senses: smell, taste, touch, and sound. Try to use literary devices in your poem so that you won't be using Metaphors or Similes too often.

"Lucy let her luck linger."
This type of writing is special and can be very effective.

Write to be heard. Poetry is made to be read out loud. Before you put the finishing touches on your poem read it out loud to check the rhyme .and meter. The test to good cooking is in the eating. The test to good writing is the reading out loud.

Get feedback from others. Share your poem. with others and solicit their opinions. Join a poetry club and ask for advice. Make every line of your poem contribute to the final project.

Use of metaphors, similes and couplets. Rhetorical devices such as simile (a likeness, where a figure of speech is likened to another: Ex. "Her tears flowed like wine.") or metaphors, (a figure of speech containing an implied comparison in which one word is compared to another, Ex." All the world is a stage.") become effective when used in poetry. Couplet, (pronounced 'keplet) is two successive lines, usually about the same length, that rhyme. (Ex. "The poem packed laughs anatomical, Into space that's quite economical.") This is used frequently in writing limericks. Using rhetorical devices make your poetry unique.

TYPES OF POETRY

Limericks.   Type of refrain is the name of a nonsense poem of five anapestic lines, often a bit bawdy, usually with rhyme scheme aabba, the first, second and fifth lines having three stresses. The third and the fourth having two. The form was popularized by Edward Lear.   Example:

> There was a young lady named Harris
> Whom nothing could ever embarrass
> Till the bath salts in the tub where she lay,
> Turned out to be plaster of Paris

Ode.   poem written to be sung, or a lyric poem, rhymed, or unrhymed, addressed to a person or thing and usually characterized by lofty feelings elaborate form and dignified style.   Example:

THE EASTER BONNET

Irving Berlin's poem the Easter bonnet typifies an ode. As he referenced the Easter parade in New York.

> "In your Easter bonnet
> With all the frills upon it,
> You'll be the grandest lady
> In the Easter parade."

Sonnet.   A poem normally fourteen lines or more with any of several fixed verse and rhythmic schemes, typically rhymed iambic pentameter. Sonnets characteristically Express a single theme or idea. **Iambic** means a verse that uses one unaccented syllable followed by one accented one. (Ex. "To strive, to seek, to find and not to yield."

FLY AGAIN

His trembling hands held the church pew that day,
Struggling to stand when they asked him to pray.
With wisdom and strength his words were spoken
But his body grew weary for his wings were broken.
But he will fly again.
He will soar with his wings unfolded:
Hear the angels applaud as he rides the wind,
To the arms of God. And he will fly again.
He will fly again.
And on that day when he left for the sky,
I saw him smile as he told me goodbye.
No more would he weep for missed tomorrow's,
No more would he suffer in the land of sorrows.
But he will fly once again.
He will soar with his wings unfolded.
Hear the angels applaud.
As he rides on the wind to the arms of God.
And he will fly, he will fly again.
I know that he is in a better place.
still dream of the day when I'll see his face.
Then we'll embrace and will fly once again
We will soar with our wings unfolded.
Hear the angels applaud.
As we ride on the wind to the arms of God.
And we will fly again.

David Phelps

Light Poetry.   Is poetry that attempts to be somewhat humorous. Light poems are usually brief and can be frivolous or serious in nature. Often light poetry features word play including puns, and adventurous rhythms.

Examples

MY MOUSE IS MISBEHAVING

My mouse is misbehaving
And my keyboard is on the fritz.
The computer is not computing
And is dropping bytes and bits.

RED

Roses are red, poppies are red
The grass in the garden is red
Darn, no wonder.
The whole State is on fire.

Biblical Poetry.   The Bible contains a number of beautiful poems. The largest book in the Old Testament is the book of Palms. With 150 chapters it is considered a book of poetry. David the celebrated King of Israel, is connected to 73 Psalms either as a writer or recipient. Other writers include Asaph, Solomon, and Moses. Psalms may be considered as entries in a dairy—they reflect people's most intimate encounters with God. When reading Psalms, one must read with your heart as well as your mind. Poetry is lasting evidence when it is connected to an event or an incident.

Elegy poetry.   Is a mournful melancholy or plaintive type poetry. It usually is a song or poem of lament or praise of the dead. Elegy may reflect something that seems to the author to be strange or different and yet is a lesson in life.

THAT FINAL DAY

It was the final day, forever.
We were standing at the gate.
Every soul was present,
Not a single person late.

St. Peter had the holy book,
And followed down the line,
As God called out the names
Each person entered one ar a time.

When God had finished,
St. Peter closed the cover tight,
One lost soul who had waited long
Cried out, "God I know you are right,
But you have somehow missed my name,
If I don't get to Heaven, it will be a shame."

Yet, God would not answer,
It was like He didn't hear.
God never missed the name,
Because the name was never there.

So, as we live our lives each day,
We need to know that God is waiting
To have the final say.
We need to have our name recorded,
In the Book of Life, the proper way.

Al Schmid

Non-sensical Poetry. Broadly defined non-sensical poetry means absurd or meaningless words telling of an act or incident that doesn't make sense. Example:

THE JOLLY OLD MAN IS GONE

Ho, ho, ho and a bottle of rum
Santa has run off to the Caribbean.
A week in the tropics and he will be alright,
Sporting a tan as he rides out of sight.

He dozed under my Christmas tree
Cuz he was here a long time.
Next year I will have cookies,
Instead of tequila shots with lime.

He was a little bit tipsy
When he staggered to his sleigh,
He was singing a Jimmy Buffett,
As he flew on his way.
It wasn't "Merry Christmas"

That he called out as he went,
It was "Mele Kalikimaka"
At least I think that's what he meant.

He was headed south the last I knew
For the land of sand and sun.
By now he is on that sandy beach,
Down in the Caribbean.

That change in latitude was on his mind,
Along with a shot or two of tequila wine.,
I'm certain that's how he forgot
The gift I had for you under my tree, fear not.
Merry Christmas and a Happy New Year
From the Jolly Old Man and me.

Steve Schmid

Narrative poetry. Is the type of poetry that tells a story. It subsumes **Epic** poetry but is usually shorter, generally with more appeal to human interest. Narrative poetry may be the oldest type of poetry.

THE BRIDGE BUILDER

An old man going along a highway
Came in the evening, cold and gray.
To a chasm vast and deep and wide,
Through which was flowing a sullen tide.
The old man crossed in the twilight dim,
The sullen stream had no fears for him.
But he turned when safe on the other side.
And built a bridge to span the tide.
Old man," said a fellow pilgrim near,
"You're wasting your strength with building here."
"Your journey will end with ending day,
"You never again will pass this way."
"You have crossed the chasm, deep and wide,
Why build you a bridge at the eventide?"
The builder lifted his old gray head,
"Good friend, in my path I have come," he said,
"There followed after me today,
A youth whose feet must pass this way,
This chasm that has been naught to me,
To the fair-haired youth may a pitfall be.
He too must cross in the twilight dim,
Good friend, I am building the bridge for him.
By giving his life for the life of the world,
Christ bridged the gulf that sin had made."

Will Allen Dromgoole

On a plaque on the Bellows Falls   Bridge in New Hampshire

Satirical poetry. Is a remarkable poetry that is used for satire. Often written for political purposes or can express sarcasm, irony, ridicule, or expose a folly or vice, or lampoon an individual. Alexander Pope, a late 17th early 18th century poet, wrote a famous poem about the "Rape of the Lock." The poem tells of an incident that occurred in English society that was made worse by a melodramatic socialite who lost a lock of her hair when a man in her circle snipped her tresses without her permission. There are a number of different subjects that address satire.

POET'S DELIGHT

Math, physics, English, and so on.
Alas are tiresome.
All the professors here go on,
With a prime axiom.

Discriminatory Poetry. Poetry written in the past may have had an element of discrimination that is likely to be unacceptable in the 21st century. In 1850 Stephen Foster wrote music and poetry that that was deemed to be improper and would be considered discretionary in today's society. As a result, his work was only played in saloons and bars. He never lived to have his music played in an opera house. An example is the poem/song *Nellie Bly*.

NELLIE BLY

Nelly Bly, Nelly Bly, bring your broom along.
Sweep the kitchen clean my dear and have a little song.
Poke the wood my lady love and make the fire burn.
And while I get the banjo down just give the mush a turn.

If Nelly Bly is a housekeeper or servant, she may feel she has been discriminated against by having to do all the chores for only a song. What's happened to the minimum wage, five- and one-half-day workweek, time and a half for overtime, 10 days sick leave and two weeks' vacation? Don't forget the allowance for uniforms and reimbursement for travel expenses. Therefore:

Nelly Bly, I know you aren't vocal, but not very shy.
The chores are done, had our song, and you didn't even cry.
It's time to tell you your benefits to help you get along.
Tomorrow's job with benefits is right where you belong.

Hey Nellie, Ho Nelly listen love to me, I'll sing for you,
And pray for you, I hope you will always stay.

Book Spine Poetry. Book Spine Poetry (BSP) is a new method of writing. BSP is a form of poetry using the titles of books printed on their spines to create freeform poems. BSP is considered a meme (an element of a culture or system of behavior that may be considered to be passed from one individual to another by non-genetic means.) Nita Khachaturian began the art in the early 1990s by stacking books so that when the titles were read on the spine, they could create short sentences and stories that became poems.

Example: Book titles

BOOK SPINE POETRY

TOMORROW'S SIGHTS AND SOUNDS

THE EYES OF A CHILD

DADDY'S GIRL

TO THE END OF THE LAND

AND SO IT IS

A THREAD OF TRUTH

Results: Tomorrow's sights and sounds
              Through the eyes of a child,
              Who is daddy's little girl,
              Is a thread of truth
              To the end of the world
              And so, it is.

BSP poetry can be done at your local library where you will find a number of different books to use. It is a whimsical way to create new poems and expand your poetry writings.

THE CHRISTIAN VIEW OF ROMANCE

There are no references to the word romance in the Bible. There are 281 times that the word *love* is used. Webster's Dictionary defines *romance* as "an ardent emotional attachment or involvement between people; a love affair." The two terms, romance and love are often used interchangeably. The true meaning of love, as defined in the scriptures, has been misinterpreted in the common usage of our English language and our society. Most often, love is confused with infatuation, or an elated high feeling we get when we fall in love. This kind of love is something that lasts typically a short time and unless replaced by true love results in broken relationships.

The Bible covers two types of love: agape and phileo. Agape love is represented by God's love for us. It is a non-partial, sacrificial love best demonstrated by the gift in John 3:16, *"For God so loved the world that He gave His only begotten Son, that whosoever believes in Him will not perish but have everlasting life." **John 3:16 NIV.*** This kind of love is unconditional. The Love Chapter in 1 Corinthians 13 deals more explicitly with love: *"Love is patient, love is kind. It does not envy, it does not boast, it is not proud. It is not rude, it is not self-seeking, it is not easily angered, and it keeps no record* of wrong *doings. Love does not delight in evil but rejoices with the truth. It always protects, always trusts, always hopes, and always preserves. Love never fails."* **1 Corinthians 13: 4-8a NIV**

This passage is often quoted at weddings and other celebrations of love.

Agape is a connection through the spirit. A true manifestation of this requires a relationship with Christ. For without Him, agape love isn't exhibited in its true form. We, as humans, can't reach this level alone. We need our Heavenly Father's Spirit in us, working through us. The spirit produces love, joy, peace, patience, kindness, goodness, faithfulness, humility, and self-control. Only through that spirit can we reach this goal.

The other love is phileo. It is considered to be brotherly love. It is usually based upon how others treat us and our feelings in any given situation. It involves direct interaction and sometimes comes with a price tag of expectation, wanting something in return. It is a demonstrative form of love offered through the soul. But it is also a command from God. *"Let us love one another, because love comes from God."* 1 John 4:7 NIV

Love is the attribute of God that means the most to us. If God didn't love us, the ones He created, He would have turned His back on us a long time ago. Despite our many failures God keeps working with us. God continues to forgive us for our sins, starting with Adam and Eve in the garden, to Abraham, Isaac, and Moses, and so many more. God loves us. He shows His love for us. He expects us to love Him totally and to show love for one another.

The relationships in our lives will be governed by agape or phileo love. When we are thinking in terms of romance, we allow agape love to pour from our hearts. As a result, we are eager to do everything we can to please the other person and make sure that person is happy. In a love relationship between a man and a woman, romance is the physical evidence of the love that exists. When that relationship progresses to marriage, the love built between the man and the woman only grows deeper as the bond is made stronger through the intimate union of body and soul. Biblical love elevates the husband's affections for his wife to the point of loving his wife, "as his own body." The Bible instructs the wives to submit to their husbands as the head of the household, but submission does not mean subservience. When agape love is shown in the marriage the couple will act as one and both will love the other as they love themselves. Tenderness and romance will come out of that love.

The best book in the Bible on romantic and agape type love is the Song of Solomon. This book demonstrates the parallel between the agape love that Christ has for the church and the abiding love that a husband needs to have for his bride.

Considering God's Word, it is important to keep in mind that **love/romance** is an action. It is not passive, and is not a feeling. It is a verb. It requires you to do something in order to make it work. It requires you to put the other person's wants and desires above your own. In order to be refreshed read 1 Corinthians 13 and let the Holy Spirit work through you.

ALL MY LIFE HAS BEEN LIKE A HOLDING PATTERN

Seems like all my life has been a holding pattern.
It's like a circle from sunrise to sundown.
The moon rises in the night till the dawn comes around.
My life has been a circle, and I cannot tell you why.
Seasons spin around again; the years keep rolling by.

It seems I have been here before, I can't remember when.
But I've got this feeling we will all be together again.
Life doesn't seem to have many straight lines,
And the road has many bends. There is no clear-cut
Beginning and we don't know the final end.

I've thought of this many time, you have done the same.
We lose each other, it's just like a children's game.
When we find each other, We recall all the memories we have.
Our enchantment in aviation is more than a passing fad.

Yes, life is like a circle, it's a holding pattern I say,
Until we get the clearance to complete the flight someday.

Al Schmid

TAKING TIME

I wonder, as I look ahead
At life's very short road,
That did I do or not do?
To ease someone's heavy load.

Has a careless word hurt the feelings?
Of a person close to me?
A word foolishly spoken,
A word I couldn't retrieve.

From birth to death the years fly
As sand before the wind.
The days flash before us,
A ticking of the clock sounds within.

So fast, so little time
In this world to do some good.
To do for my fellow human beings
All that I possibly could.

We don't need the praises
Or acclamations of others.
We get all the praise we need
By serving our sisters and brothers.

Helping one another
With kindness and love,
Giving something or ourselves
Is all God asks from above?

Al Schmid

LOOK FOR TOMORROW

We can't wait for tomorrow,
It may never come.
It seems that the right time
May never arrive for some.

Now is the time to make your mark.
To do what good we can do;
For in loving and helping others
We to ourselves are true.

Al Schmid

FALLING DOWN IN BLOOMFIELD

I do not like your falling down,
I do not like it in Bloomfield town
I do not like to spoil the season,
Even though I know the reason.

I do not like a broken arm,
I do not like to learn of harm.
I do not wish you any grief,
I do not like the beef, beef, beef.

I do not like to learn of sorrow.
Things will go much better tomorrow.
Keep a happy face, look on the pleasant things,
Enjoy the Christmas and holiday rings.

I don't like it at all.
But stand up straight and forget the fall.
Because you can't do much of anything now,
But call, call, call.

Albert F. Schmid

HAPPY LANDINGS

FALLING DOWN

I do not like your falling down.
I do not like to see you frown.
The fall from the ladder
Is just more than bad luck.
I wish you well, so when you sigh,
You can read a chapter of
The Unlimited Sky.

HAPPY LANDINGS

Albert F. Schmid

LANDINGS

We who fly for fun or as a pro,
Are always asked, "How'd your landing go?"
Three types of landings we can talk about,
The one you can walk away from.
Without any doubt.
The second landing is a bit more extreme,
You walk away, and can use the airplane again.
The third type of landing is always a secret.
No one would believe you if you ever repeat it.

HAPPY LANDINGS

Al Schmid

GOING TO THE DENTIST

Going to the dentist, the time has come.
To check those molars from crowns to the gums.
The dentist examines the conditions at best.
"We'll need x-rays and cleaning before the rest".

X-rays are easy and provide instant pictures,
The cleaning involves washing and scraping.
Along with some lectures.
Tarter develops when the sugar we eat,
Mixes with the saliva and other treats.

Brushing and flossing are fine, I cannot cheat.
Get into the habit of cleaning each time I eat.
A protocol of good dental hygiene helps our health,
Adds to our longevity including our wealth.

After the cleaning and X-rays are completed
The dentist returns and tells me what is needed.
Let's see, he says, "One, two, three, four . . .
You will likely need seven fillings or more."

Whew, that means three more trips to the dentist.
Am I up to facing this menace?
But going to the dentist is an interesting adventure,
When it's finished, I'll have a decent set of dentures.
So, smile!

Al Schmid

Albert F. Schmid

WE ARE NOT AN ACCIDENT

We are not an accident. Our birth was no mistake or mishap, and our life is not a fluke of nature, our parents may, or may not, have planned us, but **God** did. He was not surprised by our birth. In fact, He expected it.

Isaiah 44:2 says,
"I am your Creator.
You were in my care even before you were born."
and the Bible says,
"The Lord will fulfill his purpose for me."

God never does anything accidentally, and he never makes mistakes. He has a reason for everything He creates. Every plant and every animal, every living thing was planned by God, and every person is designed with a purpose in mind.

God's motive for creating each of us was His **LOVE** . . . long before He laid down earth's foundation, He had us in mind. He settled on us as the focus of His **Love**.

Have you ever thought about how you would have liked to look if you were given a choice? If God had given us a choice of how tall or how short we would like to be, or how skinny or athletic we would like to appear, or if we had dark skin, or light skin, or blonde or brunette, black or redhead hair? And what if the looks that caught our fancy as a child changed when we grew older?

Given the choice, what name would you have chosen? Tom, Dick, Harry, Jane, Sue or Nancy? My wife's grandmother was the last of nine children, and when she was born her parents didn't give her a name. They simply called her "Sis" and that was her name until she went to school and the teacher insisted that she had to have a name. She named herself **Sadie**. That doesn't happen too often now-a-days.

Thankfully, whether we like it or not, God didn't give us a choice. Instead God takes care of the **external details** while granting us the freedom to make the **internal choice**.

In Genesis, we read the **"God formed the earth . . . He did not create it to be empty but formed it to be inhabited."** Why did He bother to go to all the trouble of creating a universe and a world for us? Because God is **Love**. We were created as a special object of God's love. God made us so that He could love us.

The Bible tells us, **"God is Love."** It doesn't say **"God has love. He *is* Love.** There is perfect love in the fellowship of the Trinity, so God didn't need to create us. He wasn't lonely. He wanted to make us in order to express His love. God says, **"I have carried you since you were born; I have taken care of you from your birth. Even when you are old, I will be the same. Even when your hair has turned to gray, I will take care of you. I made you and I will take care of you."** If there was no God, we would all be accidents, the result of astronomical random chance in the universe. There would be no right or wrong, and no hope beyond our brief years here on earth. But there is a God who made us for a reason, and our lives have profound meaning. We discover that meaning and purpose only when we make God the reference point of our lives. **Romans 12:3** says **"The only accurate way to understand ourselves is by what God is and by what He does for us."** I once urged a new Christian to testify to other about the changes the Jesus had made in his life. I knew that his faith would grow and he would be encouraged if he talked with others about what being a Christian had done for him. He agreed with my suggestion and he surprised me by saying, **"I even testify to myself."** Here is how!

YOU ARE WHO YOU ARE

You are who you are for a reason
You're part of an intricate plan.
You're a precious and perfect unique design
Called God's special woman or man.

You look like you look for a reason,
Our God made no mistake.
He knit you together within the womb,
You're just what he wanted to make.

The parent you had were the ones he chose.
And no matter how you may feel,
They were designed with God's plan in mind,
And they bear the Master's seal.

Know that trauma you faced was not easy,
And God wept that it hurt you so;
But it was allowed to shape your heart
So that into his likeness you'd grow.

You are who you are for a reason.
You've been formed by the Master's rod.
You are who you are, beloved
Because there is a God.

Al Schmid

WAIT FOR THE PERFECT CONDITION

"HE WHO OBSERVES THE WIND WILL NOT SOW."
Ecclesiastes. 11;4 (NIV)

How often do we find ourselves standing at the airport gate, waiting for the airplane to be in place with the jet way perfectly positioned, the weather just right, the provisions stored aboard, the luggage loaded and the flight crew ready to make the boarding announcement? We are anxious to get underway to our planned destination. We are willing to launch out but we are dependent on someone else to complete the pre-flight and finish all of the preparations. All conditions may not always go as planned, but dreams do move forward. Our problem is we often become a little restless waiting for them to happen.

We may look out at the graying clouds or the rain that has started. Our baggage handlers don't seem to be loading the luggage as quickly as they should. The cabin attendants are just standing around talking about their last weekend in Florida, and the gate attendants seem to lack any sense of urgency. What a way to run an airline!

It is time to **stop** waiting for perfection, inspirations, permission to act, reassurance that it is going to work, someone to change, the right person to come along, the new administration to take over, an absence of risk, a clear set of instructions, more confidence, or even for the pain to go away.

Instead of saying I can't do that, or I don't have the resources, we need to know that **"necessity fuels invention."** Instead of saying I've never tried that before we need to say, let's give it a try. Instead of saying it will never get any better, we need to try it one more time. Instead of saying let someone else deal with it, we need to be ready to learn something new. Instead of saying, "It's not my job," say, "I'll be glad to take the responsibility." Instead of saying, "I can't," say, **"By God's grace I can."** I was a lad my father asked me to prepare the yard behind the house for a new lawn. It was in the fall. The yard had suffered terribly from an extremely hot and dry summer. It needed to be cultivated, racked and made ready for seeding. I worked at the task for several days thinking it would never be completed. Finally, it came

time for planting. But it was a windy, stormy day and I didn't think it wise to continue with the job.

I was reminded of the scripture: *"Whoever watches the wind will not plant; whoever looks at the clouds will not reap."* Ecclesiastes 11:4. I might add, *"Whoever sees black clouds in the sky will not fly."* When dad came home from work that night, he was not happy with my decision not to plant the seeds. He reminded me of the scripture: *"Sow your seed in the morning, and at evening let your hands be idle, for you do not know which will succeed, whether this or that, or whether both will do equally well."* Ecclesiastes 11:6.

For us to accomplish a task or to complete a project we cannot spend all of our time thinking about what must be done. Instead we need to reflect on what we have already accomplished and what we have learned from the results. Football coach John Wooden said, **"Things turn out best, for the people who make the best of the way things turn out."**

There is a strong relationship between our movement toward our dreams and the resources we need becoming available to us. Too often we want to be able to see the resources or even have them in hand before we start moving forward. When we do this, we have neither the resource or the movement.

We need to be like the snail that began climbing up an apple tree one cold wintery day. As he inched his way upward a worm stuck its head out of a crevice in the tree and said, "You are wasting your energy. There isn't a single apple on this tree." The snail kept on climbing and replied, "No, but there will be by the time I get there!"

Over and over in the Scriptures God sends his people out with what seems to be little or no resources. But when they got to where God wanted them to be, the resources needed to get the job done were in place, waiting for them. Vision does not follow resources, it happens the other way around. First, we have a dream, then we have to move toward it, and the resources follow.

A wise man once said, "Effort only releases its reward after a person refuses to quit." People who succeed see what other people don't. That is what keeps them moving forward. It was by faith that Moses lead the Israelites out of the land of Egypt, not fearing the king's anger. He kept right on going because he kept his eyes on the one who is invisible. He believed in God and he followed His directions. It wasn't easy and the Israelites were impatient and very impatient. God knew their limitations and made them wander through the wilderness for 40 long years. But at God's time they entered into the promise land.

STOP AND TAKE A BREAK

Life can make us weary and stressful most the time.
We need to ask the Lord to help our spirits shine.
Take time to bless our souls before we ever speak,
Reflect you're never ending love for every one we meet.

We give our hopes and dreams to God,
Then leave them in His hands.
We know that with Godly love you care for us,
To do what you have planned.

If I can do some good today, or help in what I say,
If by my deeds your love conveys a truly righteous way.
Dear Lord, just show me how, I will do it as I pray.

Rev. Al Schmid

A PRAYER TO CHANGE YOUR LIFE

Sometime around three thousand years ago, one of history's great nobodies decided to pray. When he looked at himself and his circumstances, he saw no reason for hope. But when he prayed, he prayed the boldest and most hopeful prayer he could imagine. And God answered him.

God is still answering. The prayer, of a man named *Jabez*, is motivating millions of people today to seek the Lord in a new way, to cry out to Him for blessings, and to reach for a larger and more full filling life in HIS service.

Too many people put off doing something that brings them joy because they haven't thought about it, or don't have it on their schedule, or didn't know it was coming or didn't think it was possible.

Someone once said there is really very little difference between people— but that *little difference --- makes* all of the difference in the World.

If you haven't read *THE PRAYER OF JABEZ, I* highly recommend that you do. If you are new to the story, you'll find it in *1 Chronicles, buried* in the official genealogies of the tribes of Israel. The historian, writing about 500 years B.C. traces the official family tree of the Jews from Adam through thousands of years up to his own time. The first nine chapters of the book are taken up with naming the names. It is the most boring book in the Bible

Suddenly in the Fourth Chapter, verse 9, one name, the forty-fourth, deserves special comment: *"Now Jabez was more honorable than his brothers, and his mother called his name Jabez, saying, "Because I bore him in pain." And Jabez called on the God of Israel saying, "Oh, that you would bless me indeed, and enlarge my territory, that YOUR hand would be with me, and that you would keep me from evil, that I may not cause pain."* **So, God granted him what he requested.** *1 Chronicles 4: 9-10*

In the next verse, the roll call continues as if nothing has happened., *Cheub, Shuah, Mehir.* You can scour from front to back in the Bible looking for more insight into this man Jabez, and you will find nothing. A simple man made a simple prayer to God and God granted him what he requested.

In Hebrew the name Jabez *means* pain. A literal rendering could read, "He causes (or will cause) pain." All babies arrive with a certain amount of pain, but *Jabez's* birth went beyond the usual. His mother could not understand it. We know simply that things started badly for a person no one had heard of: he prayed an unusual one sentence prayer; and things ended extraordinarily well.

Jabez's prayer asked for four things: (1) He asked God to Bless him. (2) He asked God to enlarge his territory, (3) He asked God to be with him....and (4) He asked God to keep him from evil so that he would not cause anyone else to have pain.

That one prayer and a life that was more honorable than his brothers, earned *Jabez* a place of honor in Israel's history books. Fortunately for us, his mini-biography reveals an intriguing record of personal transformation. If we look hard enough, we will find hiding behind each of *Jabez's request* a truth that can change our lives and our futures.

Personal change begins when you cry out to God .... *for what He wants for you*—with hands open and heart expectant. Miracles begin here. Each day you'll see new beginnings and new opportunities. You will think new thoughts. The direction of your life will shift, and your Name like *Jabez's* will be headed for God's honor roll for all of eternity.

Dear Lord, thank you for making me in your image.
Preparing me for a wonderful and important linage.
Forgive me for withdrawing into my own limiting dreams.

When I do this, I deny you the freedom to use me,
As your mouth, hands, and heart, it seems.
Let me fulfill your world-sized dream every day,
For my life with you in eternity.

I want to run into your arms hearing the words,
"Well done." true and faithful servant be,
Please expand my influence and impact for you
I am your devoted servant. Here am I Lord send me.

Al Schmid

GET UP AND GO

How do I know that my youth is all spent?
Well, my get up and go has got up and went.
But in spite of it all I am still able to grin.
When I think of the places my getup has been.

Old age is goldened I've heard it said.
But sometimes I wonder when I get out bed.
My ears in a drawer, my teeth in a cup,
My eyes on the dresser, Until I wake up.

Ere sleep dims my eyes, I say to myself,
Anything else I should put on the shelf?
And I'm happy to say as I close my door,
My friends are the same, perhaps even more.
But now I am old and conditions have come,
To where I walk slowly when I used to run.
The reason I know, my youth is all spent,
My get up and go has got up and went.

I don't really mind as I recall with a grin,
The wonderful life aviation has been.
The folks I have met, the planes I've flown,
The times I have enjoyed while away from home.

When asked if I would do it again,
My answer is brief and succinct,
The Sky is Unlimited.
What do you think?

Al Schmid

ODE TO THE WINGS OF GOLD

A Naval Aviator's wings of gold,
When pinned on his chest with pride.
Will never come off, whether seen or not,
For they are there until he dies.

Those wings, though metal, are fused to the soul.
With adrenaline, adversity and froth.
No one can deny the feelings received,
When he successfully completes the loft.

In the world of flying, a life time of stories,
Of memories of ship-mates and friends.
Feelings last long after the flights are gone,
And the duty assignments have end.

When the flight suit is hung in the closet with care,
The Wings of Gold still exist.
A Naval Aviator's bearing speaks of what was,
But his heart clearly speaks of what is.

Go Navy!

Al Schmid
USNR

A DOG NAMED LUCKY

Mary and her husband Jim had a dog named Lucky. Lucky was a real character. Whenever Mary and Jim had guests for the weekend, they would warn their friends not to leave their luggage open because Lucky liked to help himself to whatever he could reach. Inevitably, someone would forget and something would come up missing.

Lucky had a toy box in the basement and there was where all of treasures would be stashed; amid his other favorite toys. Lucky always put his finds in his toy box and he was very particular that his toys were in the box as well.

It happened that Mary found she had breast cancer. Something told her she was going to die of the disease......in fact she was sure it was fatal.

She was scheduled for a double mastectomy. She was fraught with fear. The night before she was to go to the hospital, she cuddled Lucky to her bosom. What would happen to Lucky? Although the three-year-old dog liked Jim he was very much Mary's dog. "If I die Lucky will be abandoned", she said. "He won't understand I didn't want to leave him." The thoughts made her sadder than thinking of her own death.

The surgery went well, but it was harder on Mary than her doctors had told her. Mary was hospitalized for over two weeks. Jim took Lucky for his evening walks but the little dog just drooped, whining and was generally miserable.

The day came for Mary to leave the hospital. When she arrived home, she was so exhausted she couldn't even make it up the stairs to her bedroom. Jim made his wife comfortable on the couch and left her to nap. Lucky stood watching but he didn't come to her when she called. It made Mary feel even worse. She soon dozed off to sleep.

Mary woke up suddenly. For a moment, she couldn't understand what was wrong. She couldn't move her head and her body felt heavy and hot. Then she realized what had happened. She was covered, literally blanketed, with every treasure Lucky owned. While she had been sleeping the sorrowing, dog had made numerous trips to the basement bringing his beloved mistress all his favorite things. **He had covered her with his love.**

Mary forgot about dying. Instead, she and Lucky began living again, walking and playing together. It was been 12 years now and Mary is still cancer free. Lucky? He still steals treasurers and stashes them in his toy box, but Mary remains his greatest treasure.

Moral: *Live every day to the fullest. Each minute is a blessing from God. Never forget that people who make a difference in our lives are not the ones with the most credentials, the most money or the most awards. They are the ones who always care.*

In spite of illness, in spite of handicaps, even of sorrow, one can remain alive long past the usual date of disintegration if one is unafraid of change, is filled with faith, has an un-satiable intellectual curiosity, an interest in big things and is happy in small ways,

If you see someone without a smile today give them one of yours. **Live simply, love seriously, care deeply, speak kindly, and leave the rest to God.**

None of us want to get to the end of our lives and find that we have just lived the **length** of it. We want to have lived the **width** of it as well.

A RETIREE'S LAST TRIP TO ALLIE'S FEED STORE

Yesterday I stopped at Allie's Feed store in North Kingstown to pick up a bag of Blue Seal dog food for my pet dog Fenway. Fenway is a miniature, short haired, Dachshund who weighs in at about 15 pounds. He speaks neither German nor English but is able to clearly communicate with us, especially when he is hungry.

I was in the checkout line when a woman behind me asked if I had a dog. What did she think I had? I told her I was starting the Blue Seal diet again. I added that I probably shouldn't because the last time I was on it I ended up in the hospital. I had lost 50 pounds but I ended up in the intensive care ward with tubes coming out of my orifices and an IV in both arms.

I told her that essentially it was a perfect diet and the way it works is to load your jacket pockets with Blue Seal nuggets and simply eat one or two every time you feel hungry. The food is nutritionally complete so it works well and I was going to try it again. (I must mention here that practically everyone in the line was now enthralled with my story.)

Horrified, the lady asked, "If you ended up in the hospital was it because the dog food poisoned you?" I told her no, I stopped to pee on a fire hydrant and a car hit me.

I though the guy behind her was going to have a heart attack, he was laughing so hard, Allie's said it okay to stop by any time, just be careful what you talk about. Older folks have all the time in the world to think up crazy things

FLY AGAIN

His trembling hands held the church pew that day,
Struggling to stand when they asked him to pray.
With wisdom and strength his words were spoken
But his body grew weary for his wings were broken.
But he will fly once again.

He will soar with his wings unfolded;
Hear the angels applaud as he rides on the wind,
To the arms of God, and he will fly.
He will fly again.

And on that day when he left for the sky,
I saw him smile as he told me goodbye.
No more would he weep for missed tomorrows,
No more would he suffer in this land of sorrows.

But he will fly once again.
He will soar with his wings unfolded.
As he rides on the wind to the arms of God.
And he will fly. He will fly again.

I know that he's in a better place.
I still dream of the day when I'll see his face.
Then we'll embrace, and we will fly once again.
We will soar with our wings unfolded
And we will fly. We will fly again.

Words and music by David Phelps

TAFFY WAS A COLLIE DOG

More than fifty years ago, when my five children were all young, and going to elementary school or kindergarten, we learned a poem that has stayed with us for all these years. The poem was entitled, *TAFFY WAS A COLLIE DOG.*

At the time, we were raising registered collie puppies. The kennel was often filled to over-flowing with pups. The children shared in the feeding, grooming, cleaning of the pens, and training the little fellows. It was educational for the children to learn how to raise and take care of a pet. As the kids became more and more involved with the dogs, we found a poem that fit and it was memorized by even the youngest who was in kindergarten. Taffy Was a Collie Dog.

The poem was memorable, and the children learned it quickly. Perhaps it was because the pups were all every active and full of the devil. The kids enjoyed naming each puppy and they quickly responded to their names. One beautiful little female was named Taffy. She had a full white collar, white paws, long collie nose with lovely sable and white markings. The name Taffy fit her well. The dogs all looked like Lassie, the famous dog in the movies.

The children loved her but she had her own personality. One could never anticipate what trouble she would get in or when it would happen. As a result, when this nursery rhyme was penned it stuck with Taffy. The story goes like this:

TAFFY WAS A COLLIE DOG

Taffy lived in the kennel out near the bog.
Taffy was a good dog; the children loved her brief.
Taffy was a handsome dog, but Taffy was thief.

Taffy came to my house and stole a piece of beef.
I went to Taffy's house, Taffy was not home.
Taffy came to my house and stole a marrow bone.
I went to Taffy's house, Taffy was in bed.
I picked up the marrow bone and beat her on the head.

I have often wondered why the poem was so popular with the kids. Was it because the story was about their beloved dog? Was it because they identified with the prankishness of this lovable creature? Was it because of the rhythm of the poem? Was it the violence at the end? I may never know the answers to these questions.

And so, it is with poetry; paint a picture; tell a story, make it rhyme; have it be easy to remembered; and end it with a moral line. The rappers of the 21st century use these ways to popularize their messages today. Everlasting poetry.

Schmid

WE ARE HERE FOR A REASON   62 YEARS

We are here for a purpose . . .
It may take a lifetime to occur.
We see everything in a different light,
Relationships, tasks, motives, goals or plans.
We always want to make things right.

The plan reordered was a bit incognito,
To unite and remember the times shared at Chinco.
Good years and time with our shipmates and flying.
The memories go on without even trying.

The Lord is near, not a million miles away.
Only inches from our heart, the scriptures say,
When Jesus came to the world that day,
He came as a neighbor meaning to stay.

We are blessed and can rejoice,
Because the Lord is only a breath away.
We can talk with him at night or during the day.
He wants to know what we think and pray.

Sixty-two years may be considered a lifetime for some.
But we were meant to be united, and wasn't it fun?
Thank you, Max and Reba, Charlie and Janet,
For the greatest time on this here planet.

"I cry to God Most High, to God who fulfills His purpose in me."
Psalm 57:2

Al Schmid

LIMERICKS

Limerick is a form of poetry that is non-seneschal, bawdy and often humorous. Webster defines a limerick as a refrain containing the name, a nonsense poem of five anapestic lines, often bawdy, usually with the rhyme scheme, aabba, the first, second, and fifth lines have three stresses, the third and fourth having two. The form was popularized by Edward Lear.

Examples:

For every word there's a rhyme
Which I have found in due time,
I take it to heart,
Poetic art,
And only through Limericks do they shine.

Some think that I am Albert the poet.
But others don't really know it.
Till I looked at my shoes in vain,
Longfellow, is not the name,
But the feet likely show it. Size 12."

I'm sorry these words seem rude,
But my poetry skills are too crude
Just take your chewing gum
For I am already done
And you can leave while I'm in a good mood.

Al Schmid

CONDOLENCES

Crystal (Langevin) Litchfield
March 28, 1980 – August 19, 2018

It is with a broken heart that we say farewell
To the loving mother of our two grandchildren,
Christopher and Mia Litchfield.

Crystal Langevin Litchfield you forever will be in our hearts.
Your love and gentle spirit will live on through your children and
everyone in these parts for more than a million.

Rest in peace sweet child.

Sheri Litchfield

THE NEED TO FLY

I watch as he turns to leave the hangar
His eyes scroll about as he takes it all in.
My heart feels the ties I know he is breaking,
I see a blink, then a tear as he tries to grin.

Weather, flight plans, near and far away lands,
That's how he has lived, this gentleman.
This decision, put off for so long
Says, "Let's wrap it up," that is the plan.

The love for all he is, hits me so hard,
Watching his face like a living cue card.
The list of his losses he alone must review,
Will he allow me to help him get through?

Thousands of miles across the great sky,
Loving the privilege of his own wings to fly,
Seeing the world from a lofty view,
While modestly saying, "That's what I do."

A surprise in the offing is what we both need.
Time for the grandkids, and each other indeed.
Homebodies on outings by car or by air.
It won't matter to me as long as he's there.

Leisurely outings not controlled by a clock.
A hand-hold stroll down some rustic dock.
Time to give back for all that has been,
Making room for each other away from life's din.

Albert F. Schmid

A prayer by Jabez was the very first glue.
Each was alone, but life is better by two.
This time in life may we spend it together?
This our own autumn, life's sweetest weather.
Thank God for the blessings on this our love.

Audrey C. Schmid

CURE FOR COMPLAINERS

Someone once said, "Everyone complains about the weather, but nobody does anything about it. And that seems to be the truth. Seems it is it almost like old age. Satchel Page said, "Age is mind over matter. If you don't mind it won't matter."

With the series of snow and ice storms that we have had; coupled with digging out, getting around and finding a place to park, it is enough to make us all super complainers. Then, throw in a couple days of minus temperatures, -2 at my house yesterday, and it really makes us grumble.

Philippians 2: 14-15 tells us this: *"Do all things without grumbling, or questioning. That you may be blameless and innocent children of God without blemish."*

This little jingle may help us cope:

> Little things that fret and try us,
> Causing murmur and complaint,
> If borne as He intended,
> Are the making of a Saint.
> Don't complain about weather,
> The snow and ice today,
> Be grateful for the forecast,
> Spring is on its way.

Don't pray when it rains, if you don't pray when the sun shines.

Al Schmid

GOING TO LUNCH AT THE SENIOR CENTER

Tuesdays and Thursdays have a special encounter
A wholesome lunch at the Senior Center.
Menus of Fried Chicken, Macaroni and Cheese,
Chicken Cacciatore, or Turkey Stew, if you please.

All the folks who attend are delighted to find,
The meal is a plenty, enough for all kind.
Start with juice then the main course of the day,
A garden salad and mixed vegetables, per say
Potatoes and gravy, a buttermilk biscuit.
Finish the meal with a dessert that's terrific.

Thanks to the kitchen staff who prepare the feast,
We appreciate your efforts, to say the least.
Generous servings, never attractingly lost,
Are worth a King's ransom whatever the cost.

For those over sixty we extend you this choice,
Tuesday or Thursday, lunch with your host.
The Granby Senior Center, I say
Will serve to brighten the rest of your day.

Al Schmid

A TRIP TO GRANBY CENTER

I like to get on the bus each day and see your friendly smile.
The trip to Granby Senior Center just takes a little while.
The time goes fast because we have an awful lot to say,
Who won the baseball game and leads the league today?

You are an avid Yankee fan and the BoSox's are my choice,
To each his own, the credit's due to team who wins the most.
But the baseball games last only a precious little while,
Now we follow the UConn Huskie basketball girls,
With their outstanding winning style.

We know each player's name, and where she is from.
We second-guess Coach Geno, as to how he has always won.
A winning team is a special gift, it gives UConn all the fame
But hats off to the players who work so hard to glorify the name.

Good news, the Huskies won again. We are blessed.
Now we can decorate our Holiday with total happiness.

Al Schmid

THE CHURCH, AN ORGAN, A BELL AND A CLOCK

The word church in the New Testament is *ekklesia,* which means literally the **calling out,** an assembly of a congregation or community. The word church is found only four times in the gospels; Matthew, Mark, Luke and John.

Paul the missionary, founder of many churches, created a famous metaphor that adds to the meaning of **Church.** In Romans 12:5, Paul writes: *"So in Christ we who are many forms one body."* The Church. It is not a building or a structure, but rather the act of gathering scattered people into an organic unity in Christ, making a single living organism. Paul had a very strong notion of the Christian community. He believed that the church would develop **love and unity** and that it would grow and attract new members, helping each other and strengthening one another. And so, it has.

As you think about **The Church,** perhaps you think about your favorite church. The one that is closest to your heart. Maybe it is local, maybe is it far away. It might be the church that you grew up in. Or the church in which you were baptized. It might be the church in which you were married, or the one in which your children were confirmed, or received their first communion. Such churches hold beloved memories.

One of my favorite Churches is located in Springfield, Illinois. The church in which I was married, the church that my family attended regularly and the church that offered me such wonderful opportunities to be of service. South Side Christian Church

There is a Church in Washington, D.C. which is a famous historical church. It is the **Calvary Baptist Church** of Washington. It is an old church, built in 1886, famous for it preaching, its great congregations and its effect on the nation's Capital. Its history goes back to the days of Andrew Jackson and Martin Van Buren.

When the congregation was called together to build the church building there was a man by the name of Amos Kendall who was instrumental in raising the monies needed to build the church. He was a financial advisor to Samuel Morse, the inventor of the telegraph and although he never joined the church he gave generously to its growth. But Amos Kendall had three stipulations:

1. The Church must have an organ.
2. The Church must have a bell,
3. The Church must have a pulpit clock.

Each stipulation had a symbolic reference.

The **organ** was a mighty instrument. On it was played thunderous anthems and melodious hymns. With the many keys on the organ console each represented a certain pitch or tone that made harmony and rendered a beautiful message. Let one key not play or get stuck and it might make the tune offensive and unpleasant to the ear. And so the message that we receive is portrayed as keys of the organ, we need to function in harmony and in unity.

The **bell** is another symbol. It was used as a call to worship. First the ringing of the bell was an invitation to come to worship. The second ringing affirmed that the people had assembled.

The bell was also an invitation to get ready for a joyous wedding, a new birth or to memorialize a death in the family. It was also used as a fire alarm calling the volunteers to come and fight the fire. The bell proclaims God's word and rings out the conviction of religious freedom.

Oscar Hammerstein, after being diagnosed with cancer went to Mary Martin's dressing room during the performance of **Sound of Music** and added these words to her famous song:

"A bell is no bell till you ring it.

A song is no song till you sing it.

Love in your heart wasn't put there to stay,

Because love isn't love till you give it away."

Symbolism of the **clock.** I know some preachers who would rather not have to look at a pulpit clock. They want to keep talking. But the clock reminds us we don't have forever to serve God while in this world. When the moment passes it is gone. We are called to be Christ's representative now and not later. In Frankenmuth, Michigan, a town that has been built to represent a Bavarian Village, there is a large tower clock in the town square. On the hour the clock doors open and outcome carvings of musicians and dancers who dance and swirl as the clock strikes the hour. One day a young girl and her mother were watching....out came the characters, the clock began to strike......9 –10- 11- 12- but it didn't stop, 13 – 14 - 15...and the little girl took her mother's hand and said, "**Mommy is it later than it has ever been before.**" And so, it is.

Amos Kendall's stipulations were prophetic. The **organ** does symbolize the harmony and unity that is needed in the Church, in our lives and in our relationships. The **Bell** proclaims peace and love that we receive from God. The **Clock** is a constant reminder that now is the time to be God's servant.

May the gifts and symbols be forever in our hearts and in our minds.

CHOOSING IS EASIER WHEN YOU UNDERSTAND THE RESULTS

"For God so loved the world that he gave his one and only son that whoever believes in him shall not perish but have everlasting life." John 3: 16

The church was nearly filled to capacity Sunday evening. After having sung several hymns the minister went to the pulpit and before he started his sermon, he paused to introduce a guest minister, who was attending the service.

The Pastor told the congregation the guest minister was one of his dearest childhood friends and he wanted him to take a few moments to greet the church members and to share whatever he felt would be appropriate for the service.

Following the introduction an elderly man stepped up to the pulpit and began to speak. He said:

"A father and his son and a friend of his son went sailing off the New England coast one evening. As they sailed, a fast-moving storm approached the craft, the wind began to blow harder and harder, the sea became very rough, the waves were so high that they could not return to the harbor. Even though the father was an experienced sailor he could not keep the boat upright and the three people on board were swept into the ocean as the boat capsized."

The old man hesitated . . .made eye contact with two teenagers who were for the first time in the service beginning to seem somewhat interested in the story. The speaker continued: "Grabbing a rescue line, the father had to make the most excruciating decision of his life. To which boy should he first throw the line? He had only seconds to make a decision. The father knew that his son was a Christian and he knew the other boy was not. The agony of his decision could not be matched by the torrent of the rain and raging waves. He had to throw the line, he had to make a choice.

"The father yelled out, 'I love you son!' Then he threw the rope to his son's friend. By the time he had pulled the friend back to the capsized boat, his son had disappeared beneath the water. His body was never recovered."

By this time, the two teenagers in the pew were sitting straight up anxiously waiting for the next words to come out of the mouth of the old minister.

"The father," the preacher continued, "Knew his son would step into eternity with Jesus, but he could not bear the thought of his son's friend having to spend forever in damnation. He had sacrificed his own son in order to save the son's friend."

How great is the love of God that he should do the same for us? Our Heavenly Father sacrificed his one and only son that we could be saved. I urge you to accept His offer to rescue you by taking hold of the life-line that He is throwing to you.

Finished with his story the old minister turned and sat down in his chair. Silence filled the room. Then the young minister went to the pulpit and delivered a brief sermon, followed by a benediction.

Within minutes the two teenagers, who were so attentive, were at the old man's side. "Nice story," said the first teen, "But I don't think it was very realistic for a father to give up his only son's life in hope that the other boy would become a Christian."

"Well, you've got a point there," answered the old man as he glanced at his old worn Bible. "But I am standing here today to tell you that story to illustrate what it must have been like for God to give up his son for me."

"You see, I was the father and your minister was my son's friend."

I would rather live my life as if there is a God and die to find out there isn't, than live my life as if there isn't a God and die to find out there is.

GET WELL SOON

Its winter weather and the season is here,
To suffer the discomforts, we often bear.
Coughs and sniffles, and even the flu.
Aren't easy to have, especially for you.

The old rule-of-thumb is quite simple,
Three days arriving, three days of pain,
Then three more days to recover again.

Drink lots of water, and hot lemonade,
A tablet, an aspirin or even Tylenol aids.
It will help you with you're feeling better,
In spite of the snow and lousy weather.

Take it easy and don't get shook,
Get lots of rest and read a good book.
Keep me posted on your wellbeing,
I'm looking forward to a happy ending

Get well soon

UNCOMFORTABLE PILLOWS

"For He gives sleep to his beloved." Psalm 127:20

I had returned from a trip to the Midwest to attend a high school reunion number 66. Class of 1946 and '47 have had a reunion every year since 1949. I went for two reasons; one of course, was to see and visit with my old friends of 65 years, many had passed on. The alum's total had shrunk, but 46 members were present. The other reason for going was to see my younger brother whom I hadn't seen in six years. My original plan was to drive to Springfield, Illinois but after I checked my GPS I remembered the distance was 963 miles from my driveway to Charlie's house. It was then that I began feeling my age and chose to fly. It was a great flight with only one connection and the enroute time was less than 6 hours. Much better than two days of driving.

One of the things that I noticed at the airline terminal was the passengers of today are much different than they were 25 years ago. Seems like casual attire is the norm. Everyone has carried luggage, a duffel bag or a back pack. One man sitting near me pulled out a small pillow and promptly went to sleep. I was reminded of the times when our family traveled and how my youngest son always insisted on taking his pillow with him to grandmother's house. It wasn't that she didn't have large, comfortable downy pillows, it was something that Shane liked and felt he wanted his own pillow. A security blanket, a remembrance of home, it had a comforting effect on his traveling. We of course, let him have his way.

There are many people who do the same thing today. They wouldn't think twice of traveling somewhere without their pillow. They want to sleep well. Maybe that is why the Bible story of Jacob challenges me. Genesis 28: 10-20 NIV. Tells of Esau, Jacob's brother, son of Isaac who had learned that their father had blessed Jacob and sent him to Paddan Aram to take a wife. Isaac commanded Jacob not to marry a Canaanite woman. When Esau found out what had happened, he became very angry and he promptly went out and married two more women in addition to the wives he already had. He was angry with his father and with his brother.

Jacob was fleeing from his brother Esau. There were no Holiday Inns or Motel Sixes, who leave the light on, for him. There wasn't even a relative's home or friend's apartment that Jacob could use. Jacob had to sleep under the stars with a stone for a pillow. It's safe to say that this may have been the most uncomfortable pillow one would ever have. Yet despite his physical discomfort he believed in the almighty God. One night as he slept on the stone, he had a dream in which God appeared to him and blessed him. When Jacob awoke, he transformed the stone into a pillar and called it Bethel---God's house. We too, can sleep peacefully in the midst of uncomfortable circumstances knowing God is with us. What we must do is to give God our discomfort and expect a blessing. Whatever may keep us awake at night we need to give it to God and ask for His blessing. He can make soft pillows out of stones.

THE BRIDGE BUILDER

An old man going along a highway
Came in the evening, cold and gray.
Through which was flowing a sullen tide.
The old man crossed in the twilight dim,
The sullen stream had no fears for him.
But he turned when safe on the other side.
And built a bridge to span the tide.
"You are wasting your strength with
"Your journey will end with ending day,
You never again must pass this way."
You have crossed the chasm, deep and wide,
Why build you a bridge at the eventide?"
The builder lifted his old gray head,
"Good friend, in my path I have come,"
There followed after me today,
A youth whose feet must pass this way,
This chasm that has been naught to me,
To the fair-haired youth may a pitfall be,
He too must cross in the twilight dim,
My friend, I am building the bridge for him.
By giving his life for the life of the world,
Christ bridged the gulf that sin had made."

Will Allen Dromgoole

ANOTHER DOG STORY

While driving through the back woods of Montana a man saw a sign in front of a broken-down shanty farm house. The sign read, **"TALKING DOG FOR SALE."** The man was curious so he stopped and rang the bell. The owner came to the door and when asked if he had a talking dog replied, "Yep! He is in the back yard."

They went to the back-yard and there sat a nice-looking Golden Labrador retriever. "Do you talk?" asked the man. "Yep," the dog replied. After the man recovered from the shock of hearing the dog talk, he said, "So what is the story?" Tell me about how you learned to talk.

The Lab looked up and replied, "Well, I discovered I could talk when I was pretty young. I wanted to help the government so I called the CIA. In no time they had me jetting from country to country, sitting in rooms with world leaders and intelligence people because no one figured I would be eavesdropping. I was one of CIA's most valuable spies. After several years all the travel really worn me out, and I wasn't getting any younger so I decided to come home and settle down."

"I got a job at the airport with TSA as an undercover security agent. I would wander around near suspicious travelers and listen to their conversations and I uncovered some incredible dealings. I was awarded a batch of medals. After that I got married and had a mess of puppies. Now I am retired."

The man was utterly amazed. He turned to the farmer and asked, "What do you want for the dog?"

"Ten dollars," the farmer said. "Ten dollars?" The man exclaimed. "Why on earth are you selling him so cheap?" "Because he is a liar. He ain't never did any of that stuff," replied the farmer.

Proverbs speaks clearly of the matter of lying. *"Truthful lips endure forever, but a lying tongue is but for a moment. Deceit is in the heart of those who devise evil, but those who plan honesty have joy. No ill befalls the righteous but the wicked are filled with trouble. Lying lips are an abomination to the Lord, but those who act faithfully are his delight." Proverbs 12: 19-22*

We learn quickly that lying requires a lot of skill. Once a lie is perpetrated it requires additional lies to support it. Each step-in support of the first falsehood becomes increasing more difficult to sustain.

"The lips of the righteous know what is acceptable but the mouth of the wicked learn what is perverse."

Proverbs 10: 32 (NIV)

THE GOSPEL MESSAGE SIMPLY STATED

The Good News refers to the teaching of Jesus Christ and the Apostles. The New Testament books, Matthew, Mark, Luke and John are called the Gospels. Each contains many stories and examples from which we can learn how to live a righteous, meaningful and happy life. However, there are other sources that are available in order to learn these essential lessons. The following story is a wonderful lesson, for all of us.

The story: Carl was a quiet man. He didn't talk much and stayed pretty much to himself. But he would always greet you with a smile and a firm handshake. Carl lived in the same neighborhood for more than 50 years but no one could really say that they knew him.

Before his retirement he took the bus to work each morning. The sight of him walking down the street often worried the neighbors. He had a slight limp from a wound that he had received in WWII. The neighbors feared that although he had survived the War he may not be safe in the changing downtown environment. The area had become infested with acts of crime, random violence, gang activity and drug dealing. It was happening in every large city.

When Carl saw an announcement in the Sunday Church Bulletin asking for volunteers to help care for the gardens around the Church, he responded without hesitation. In his characteristically quiet, but unassuming way, Carl took the job. No fanfare, he just signed up.

Carl was eighty-seven years of age. It wasn't long before the very thing that his friends feared happened. He was watering the garden one day when three punk-gang members approached him. Ignoring their attempts to intimidate him Carl simply asked, "Would you like a drink of water from the hose?" The tallest and toughest looking of the three said, "Yeah old man, I'll have a drink." Carl offered the hose to him but the other two grabbed his arm throwing him to the ground. As the hose snaked crazily over the ground it doused everything in its way.

Carl's assailants grabbed him and stole his retirement watch and his wallet, and away they ran.

Carl tried to get up but he had been thrown down on his bad leg. He lay there trying to help himself as the minister came running to help. "Carl are you okay?" asked the minister. "Are you hurt?" he kept asking as he helped him to his feet. Carl passed a hand over his brow and sighed, shaking his head. "Just some punk kids. I hope they will wise up someday."

His wet clothes clung to his slight frame as he bent down to pick up the hose. He re-adjusted the nozzle and began to water. Confused and a little concerned the minister asked, "Carl, what are you doing?" "I've got to finish my watering," was the reply, "It's been very dry lately." Satisfied that Carl was all right the minister could only marvel at what had happened. He believed that Carl was fine. He was a man from a different time and different place.

A few weeks went by and the three punks returned. As was the case the first time, they began to intimidate Carl. Carl did not over react. He again offered them a drink from the hose. This time they didn't rob him but they wrenched the hose from his hands and drenched him from head to foot with icy water. When they had finished their assault, they sauntered off down the street laughing and yelling catcalls and profanity. Carl just watched them go. Then he turned towards the warm sunshine, picked up his hose and went back to work.

The summer was quickly fading into fall. Carl was doing some tilling around the shrubs when he was startled by someone coming up from behind. He stumbled and fell into the evergreens. As he struggled to regain his footing, he turned to see the leader of the punk-group reaching down for him. He braced himself for the expected attack.

"Don't worry old man, I'm not going to hurt you this time," he said. The young man spoke very softly offering his help. Carl got up. The young man reached into his pocket and slowly pulled out a crumpled bag and handed to Carl. "<u>What is this?</u>" asked Carl. "It is all of your stuff," the man explained, it's all of the stuff we took including your wallet and your money." "I don't understand," Carl said, "Why would you help me now?"

The man shifted his feet, seemly embarrassed and very comfortable, as he began to speak. "I learned something from you" he said. "I ran with that gang and hurt people like you. We picked on you because you were old and we knew we could get away with it. But every time we came and did something to you, instead of yelling and fighting back you offered us a drink of water. You didn't hate us for tormenting you. You kept showing love in spite of what we did. The young man stopped for a moment, sighed and said, "I couldn't sleep after we stole your stuff so I'm bringing it back." He paused for another moment, not knowing what to say, and finally he said, "That bag is my way of saying thanks for straightening me out." Then he turned and walked away.

Carl looked at the bag in his hands and gingerly opened it. He took out his gold retirement watch and put it back on his wrist. He opened the wallet and checked his wedding picture. He grazed for a moment at the young bride who smiled back at him after all those years.

Carl died a couple of days before Christmas. Many of his friends came to calling hour and to the funeral. At the service the minister noticed a tall young man, who he didn't recognize, sitting quietly in the rear corner of the church. During the sermon the minister spoke of **Carl's Garden, A Lesson in Life.** In a voice made with thick unshed tears he said, "Do your best and make your garden as beautiful as you can. We will never forget Carl's garden."

The following spring another announcement was made in the Sunday bulletin, it read, Person **needed to care for Carl's Garden.** The announcement went unheeded by members of the church until one day there was knock on the Pastor's door. Opening the door, the minister saw a man he thought he recognized. "I believe this is my job, if you will have me," the young man said.

The young man went to work and over the next several years he tended the flowers and shrubs just like Carl had done. During that time, he finished high school, went on to college, and even got married. He joined in the community projects and became a leader in his hometown. He never forgot his promise to Carl's memory and kept the garden just like Carl would have done.

One day the young man came to see the minister and explained that he could no longer care for the gardens. He said with a shy and happy smile, "My wife just had a baby boy and we are bringing him home tomorrow." "Congratulations," said the minister as he accepted the keys to the garden shed. "That is wonderful! What is the baby's name?" "Carl, we named him Carl." he replied.

That is the whole Gospel Message, simply inspired.

QUOTEABLE QUOTES

"The great thing in this world is not so much where we stand, but in what direction we are moving."

Oliver Wendell Holmes

"If you want to see the sun shine…. you have to weather the storm."

Frankie Lane

The way to happiness: "Keep your heart free from hate, your mind free from worry, Live simply, expect little, give much. Fill your life with love. Scatter sunshine. Forget self, think of others. Do as you would be done."

Norman Vincent Peale

"One day, in retrospect, the years of struggle will strike you as having been the most beautiful."

Sigmund Freud

"The greatest part of our happiness depends on our disposition and not on our circumstances."

Martha Washington

"He who forgives, ends the quarrel."
"It takes a minute to find a special person
An hour to appreciate them.
A day to love them.
But an entire life to forget them."

Anonymous

"Obstacles are those frightening things that you see when you take your eyes off the road."

Henry Ford

"Enthusiasm finds the opportunities, energy makes the most of them."

"It is vital that people count their blessings in order to appreciate what they have, without having to undergo actual loss."

"After the phrase, **TO LOVE......TO HELP....** is the most beautiful phrase in the world."

"One can acquire everything in solitude.... except character."

Henry Steinhart

He who has not Christmas in his heart...will never find it under a tree."

Roy Smith

"I would remind you that extremism in the defense of liberty is not vice, and let me remind you also that moderation in the pursuit of justice is no virtue."

Barry Goldwater, U.S. Senate

Albert F. Schmid

"You are my friend when you can guard my failures, Challenge my thoughts, and celebrate my success."

John Adams

Patience and perseverance have a magical effect before which difficulties disappear and obstacles vanish."

"With hurricanes, tornados, wild fires, Tsunamis, mud slides, flooding, severe earth quakes, severe thunder-storms tearing up the country from coast to coast, and the threat of swine flu, terrorist attacks and bridges falling down, are we sure this is a good time to take God out of our schools, In *God We Trust* off our coins and remove God from the Pledge of Allegiance?"

Jay Leno

A true friend is someone who knows you're a good egg, even if you are a little cracked.

BELIEVE

- There are at least two people in this world that you would die for.
- At least 15 people in this world love you in some way.
- The only reason anyone would ever hate you is because they want to be just like you.
- A smile from you can bring happiness to anyone, even if they don't like you.
- Every night someone thinks about you before they go to sleep.
- You mean the world to someone.
- You are special and unique.
- Someone that you don't even know exists loves you.
- When you make the biggest mistake ever, something good comes from it.
- When you think the world has turned its back on you, look again.
- Always remember the compliments you receive, forget the rude remarks.

Good friends are like stars. You don't always see them, but you know that they are always there.

"Whenever God closes one door, He always opens another, even though there may be Hell in the hallway."

No one falls in love by choice, it is by chance.
No one stays in love by chance, it is by work.
No one falls out of love by chance, it is by choice.

Matthew 10:32 *"Whoever acknowledges Me before men, I will acknowledge him before My Father in Heaven. But whoever disowns me before men, I will disown him before my Father in heaven"*

BENEDICTION

I would rather have one rose and kind words
From a friend while I am here,
Than a whole truck load when I'm gone.
Happiness makes you sweet,
Trials make you strong.
Sorrows keep you mounting
Failures keep you humble
Success keeps you going
But only God keeps you steady
Worry looks all around
Sorrow looks back,
Faith looks up,
Where Love abounds.

Al Schmid

DO ANGELS HAVE WINGS

Artists often paint pictures of angels having wings. People have written stories that describe angels having wings or earning their wings. But the Bible doesn't say that all angels have wings. It does say that angels can fly and that, at times, they appear with wings. But angels don't need wings to fly like birds or butterflies do. God made sure that they can get to where they are needed, when they need to go.

In the book of Daniel, we find this scripture: *"I (Daniel) prayed and Gabriel flew swiftly to me. He is the angel I had seen in the earlier vision." Daniel 9: 21*

Isaiah reported this in his scripture: *"I saw the Lord seated on a throne, high and exalted, and the train of his robe filled the temple. Above him were the seraphs (angels), each with six wings: With two wings they covered their faces, with two they covered their feet and with two they were flying." Isa. 6: 1-2.*

With this description, we might conclude that angels do have wings. Some questions we might ask would be: Why do Angels fly? Do Angels look like the ones we make in the snow? Do all angels have wings?

Finally, if we look up the word angel in the dictionary, we will find the definition: **angel (n) is a messenger of God, pictured with wings.**

HAPPY 90TH BIRTHDAY NANCY

I hope that aren't too tired
To enjoy your special day.
There are 365 days in one-year,
Times 90, is 32,850 ways.
That is a lot of living.
What more can I possibly say?
I like it when a birthday comes
It is even better when it's a
Nonagenarian one. (90th)
You have reached a special goal,
God bless you always, oh my soul.
Now that you have reached that point in life
I pray you'll continue to love and cherish
Your beautiful family and friends so nice.

**Paul says, "Though outwardly we are wasting away,
yet inwardly we are being renewed day by day."
2 Cor. 16**

Al Schmid

FLYING LOOKING UP

There are many interesting facts and trivia about flying. It has been a little more than 114 years ago that the Wright brothers flew the first fixed wing, engine powered airplane. One has to be amazed at the advancement of technology that has evolved from the first light at Kitty Hawk, North Carolina where the first flight made was for a distance of less than the wing span of our modern Boeing 747 airliner.

Now we have new large Air Bus and Boeing airplanes powered by four Rolls-Royce Trent engines that develop 10,000 pounds of thrust and the airplanes weigh **one million 250,000 pounds.** They are able to climb to 41,000 feet and cruise at a speed of .87 Mach, or 600 mph.

The airplane can carry 800 passengers for distance of 9400 miles with all of the amenities and comforts known to mankind. The runway requirements at gross takeoff weight for the A-380 Air Bus is 9,023 feet. Nearly two miles in length. In comparison, a corporate Gates-Learjet L-35 can carry 8 to 10 passengers for a distance of 2300 miles and needs a runway of less than 5,000 feet. Its cruising speed is 500 mph.

A Sikorsky S-76 helicopter can carry 6 passengers from a landing pad to its destination at 250 mph at a distance of 300 miles. And so it is with modern aviation.

However, do you know that if you put a **buzzard** in a pen that is 6 feet by 8 feet in diameter and open at the top, the bird in spite of its ability to fly, will not take off. The reason is the buzzard always begins its takeoff with a ground run of 10 to 12 feet. It will not attempt to fly without that much room. It will remain a prisoner for life, even though there is no top on its enclosure.

A **bat** flies a round at night, a blind but remarkably nimble creature in the air. But a bat cannot takeoff from a level place. If it is placed on the floor it will shuffle around helplessly until it reaches a spot that has some elevation. Then it can throw itself into the air in a flash. Or should I say, "Like a bat out of Hell."

A **bumble bee** dropped into an open glass tumble will be there until it dies, unless it taken out. It never sees the way to escape by flying out the top, but persistently keeps trying to get out through the glass at the bottom. It will keep up until it destroys its self.

People in many ways are like the buzzard, the bat and the bumblebee. They struggle with their problems and frustrations never realizing all they need to do is **Look Up.** Therein lies the answer. **Sorrow looks back. Worry looks around. But Faith looks up.**

RIDING ON THE SENIOR BUS WITH MARY

I like to get on the bus to see your friendly smile.
The trip to Granby Senior Center just takes a little while.
The time goes fast because we have an awful lot to say,
Who won the baseball game and leads the league today?

You are an avid Yankee fan, the BoSox's are my choice,
To each his own, we credit the team who wins the most.
But the baseball games last only a precious little while,
Now we follow the UConn Huskie basketball girls,
With their outstanding winning style.

We know each player's name and where she is from.
We second-guess Coach Geno, how he has always won?
A winning team puts UConn in the national Hall of Fame
Hats off to the girls who work so hard to glorify its name.

Good news, the Huskies won again. We are blessed.
Now we can decorate our Holiday with total happiness.

A Schmid

HOLIDAY GREETINGS

Holidays mean different things to many different folks.
Christmas cards, Christmas wreaths. Trees and fancy books.
I enjoy the different culinary skills that usually are forth coming.
Hot Cross buns, fancy cookies and Thomas Jefferson Bread Pudding.
I like the Christmas Spirit. It doesn't matter where you go.
Sandy beach, or Island Reach or even mountain snows.
Try to remember this advice, it really is quite free
If you don't have the Christmas Spirit in your heart,
You won't find it under the tree.
I enjoy a positive demeanor.
Our meeting for lunch at the Senior Center
Is an event that we simply enjoy, it's so refreshing.
I am always curious as what new book you are reading.
Something new at every meeting.

Paul writes in 2 Corinthians: *"Though outwardly we are Wasting away, yet inwardly we are being renewed day after day." 2 Cor. 16*

Al Schmid

Albert F. Schmid

MERRY CHRISTMAS 2018

Where has the old year gone? It is nearing Christmas and there is so much to do. Sheri and Dave are beginning to decorate the house and other than an early winter snow storm and some cold weather I am struggling to get into the Christmas spirit. I thought that writing the traditional Christmas letter might help.

2018 has been a wonderful year. I finished the book *The Unlimited Sky* and did some traveling while Sheri and Dave made their cruise to Alaska. While they were gone, I was able to go to Illinois to visit Charlie and Janet. While there I was delighted to have Max and Reba Livingston come up from Little Rock, AR to have a reunion after 62 years of faithful friendship. What a blessing it was. Charlie and I went down to Cereal Springs, IL to visit Jane and Ed. Both are enduring the aging process graciously.

On return to Connecticut I moved into my camper trailer at Scott's house in Windsor Locks. I thoroughly enjoyed the time while Sheri went to Michigan to help Kylee with her new daughter, Kinley. Number 16 great-grand daughter. The family continues to grow with Shanan and Steve Moore expecting again in February. I am eternally grateful to Scott and Shane who have helped me with fixing the squawks on the camper. It is fully winterized and ready for next season.

Audrey is still at the nursing home in East Greenwich, Greenwich Bay Manor. Her Alzheimer's condition is about the same. Drop her a card if you will.

I wish each and all a Merry Christmas and a Happy New Year. God is good!

Al Schmid

Roses are red
Violets are blue
There are lots of poems
What can I do?

The end.

Ingram Content Group UK Ltd.
Milton Keynes UK
UKHW012002100323
418413UK00005B/12